Voice of the Hawk Elder

by *Seneca Wisdomkeeper*

Edna Gordon

with Harvey Arden

Illustrations by David A. Gordon

Layout & design by George Blitch

HYT Publishing

Hawk Elder Edna Gordon

Walk Tall
Seneca
Edna Gordon 1871

Voice of the Hawk Elder

Copyright © 2006 by Edna Gordon
& Harvey Arden
Edited and compiled by Harvey Arden
Layout and Design by George Blitch
Illustrations by David A. Gordon
Photos courtesy of the Gordon family
Published by HYT Publishing
All Rights Reserved

Permission to reproduce or transmit in any form (other than educational or book review purposes) or by any means, electronic or mechanical, including photocopying and recording, or by any information storage and retrieval system, must be obtained by writing to the publisher at the address below:

HYT Publishing
c/o George Blitch
PO Box 841912
Houston, TX 77284
www.haveyouthought.com
george@haveyouthought.com

Contact Edna Gordon at: rdgordon@hotmail.com

THE AUTHOR

Edna Gordon, *Ye-o'l-wa* (Her Words), also called Grandmother Gordon, and *Ga'ya no: Se'* (New Tracks), are names handed down by generations thru' the Hen Hawk Clan. Gordon's late husband, Edwin, *Ga-Ha'da Gay-e-hoh* (Forest Garden), came from the Wolf Clan. Together they raised four children. Edna lives on the Cattaraugus Indian reservation, also known as *Deo-geh-koh* (Place of Nourishment).

Edna's writings and teachings are linked strongly to Nature and the traditional way of life. The Great Spirit has blessed her with a talent to touch the hearts of her brothers and sisters. In reading Edna's poetry and teachings we are bonded together in Unity and Spirituality.

TABLE OF CONTENTS

Dedication	7
Editor's Foreword	9
Introduction	15

POETRY

Seeing with Visionary Eyes	19
If I Had Never Been Born	20
Mother Earth's Abundant Blessings	21
Place of Friendship	22
Spellbound	23
Facing The Within	24
My Ancestral Pride	25
Wings of Prayer	26
Wolf Spirit of Wisdom	27
Hawk Trail of Wisdom	28
Words of Wisdom	30
I Shall Remain Indian	31
Wolf Hawk	32
Accept The Shadow-Side Within	35
A Child's Prayer	39
My Mis-Matched Moccasins	42
Life Is A River We Swim In	50
Wasting Time	52
Gifts We Squander	54
Signs of Love	56
An Old Woman's Earthwalk	57
To The Indian Youth of Tomorrow	63
A Broomstick Revolution	70
Respect To an Ancient Mountain	74
A Message to the Runners	75
To All Readers	85

Dedication

We dedicate this teaching book
"Voice of the Hawk Elder"
to all who desire to follow a stream of
awareness to reinforce Life's
foundation for future growth
through knowing, accepting, and
practicing the ideals of Earth Law for
inner Peace, a moral connection to
Earth, soil and spirit, and to preserve
an Earth-connected Identity for the
future generations.

Edna Gordon and Harvey Arden

EDITOR'S FOREWORD
Harvey Arden

"**W**ELCOME TO MY UMBRELLA TREE," says Hawk Elder Edna Gordon, seating herself opposite me at her well-weathered backyard picnic-table, gesturing with a wide sweep of her hand at the rich tapestry of overhanging branches which arch all the way to the ground around us, creating a kind of natural gazebo.

She nods at the tree as at a cherished old friend, and nods at me, her visitor.

"This old tree's the whole of Creation, you know, if you got eyes to see...," she says, and her throaty voice trails away thoughtfully.

I look upward into the drooping canopy of heavily leafed branches all but encasing us.

"Like a house of leaves," I say.

"More'n that," she says, "...the whole Creation's right here in this tree, if you can see it... You're sittin' right inside o' Creation itself! Don't you see it? Can't you feel it?"

I put the palm of my hand on the rough bark of the trunk.

"I ...I can feel it, I think," I say.

"Your hand on the tree, that's Life on Life," Edna says. "This Umbrella Tree here's at the center of the Universe! And so are we!"

CERTAINLY, when you're with a visionary like Edna Gordon, the Universe, the Creation itself, occupies not the background of your consciousness but the foreground. She's continually reminding me—and all of us—of the oft-forgotten fact that *We Exist! that the World, the Universe, the very Creation itself* is here and now with us at every magical instant—and that it's our privilege, our joy, and our duty as living beings to realize this in every conscious moment, to see it, to appreciate it, to be ever-thankful and ever-marveling at all of this unthinkable vastness and infinite particularity around us and within us. She insists that we see—and, yes, *feel*—this miracle that we ourselves are an integral, even essential part of this Mystery beyond all mysteries.

"Yep, it's all a Mystery. A Holy Mystery," Edna says, "No matter how far you look, that's all you're ever going to find at the end of your lookin'—a Holy Mystery."

"But how are we individual human beings essential to that Mystery….?" I ask.

Edna smiles that radiant smile of hers. With her bare toe tip she lightly taps a tiny bloom in the grass at her foot.

"Is a flower essential to the Universe?" she asks, "Some folks'll tell you, '*Oh, no It's just a flower! It lives and dies in a day or two. What does Creation need that silly little flower for?*' "

"Well, I tell you, that little tiny flower…you see it there by my toe…that little white one, no bigger than a lady's earring…That flower is essential—that's *right*,

I'm telling you, *essential*—to the whole wide Universe, same as you and me and everybody else. We're ALL essential to Creation, each and every one of us!

"Why, without that tiny little flower there it'd be a *different* Universe, a different Creation, not this one we have. D'you understand? So *THAT*'s a mighty power, don't you think? One little flower can change the entire World! Just like one person can!"

She chuckles, amused at her thought.

SOME might see a 'quaint little old lady' here. But of Edna Gordon I can tell you from years of personal observation: *quaint she ain't*. No, in this diminutive octogenarian, (maybe 5'2 on her stretched-taut tiptoes) I see a fearless warrior against injustice, a bold partisan on behalf of Mother Earth, an implacable defender of her People and of ALL indigenous Peoples.

I see her also as a natural-world philosopher, or Wisdomkeeper, a kind of *aboriginal existentialist*, seeing the inexplicable Mystery of Existence in the simplest, most 'ordinary' things—a tiny flower, a red-tailed hawk in flight, a sudden summer windstorm whipping the treetops. To Edna, these 'gifts of Creator' inspire a truly spiritual joy and an infinite thankfulness at being a conscious living presence in the very midst of the enigma of Creation. She radiates that wonder, that devout appreciation, that thankfulness in every word of this little book..

I **FIRST MET EDNA GORDON** some five or six years ago, when I was trying to create a website—

for the *Dreamkeepers Project*—that would be the digital portal to an ever growing constellation of personal websites for and by indigenous Elders. Its motto was "*Bringing the Elders to the World & the World to the Elders.*"

Itself the successor to the *Wisdomkeepers Project*, *Dreamkeepers* was to be the culmination of more than a quarter-century traveling among and working with indigenous peoples, begun while a staff writer for 23 years at National Geographic magazine, and continuing after my 1991 'retirement' in such trade books as Wisdomkeepers: *Meetings with Native American Spiritual Elders* and *Dreamkeepers: A Spirit-Journey into Aboriginal Australia.*

One day I answered the phone. A rough-gravel woman's voice said: "You Harvey Arden? This is Edna Gordon. I got some books for you to publish…"

"You do? Books you say? How many books?"

"Oh, maybe ten, maybe thirty."

"*Hmmm…* Really! *Paper* books? I'm trying to create a website for the Elders, but I've never published a book—though I've had half a dozen of my own books published. You're maybe talking about a digital online book?"

"Nope, a REAL paper book! I got thirty of'm. Maybe forty!"

"Already published?"

"Had'm printed myself. Got a few copies each. Whaddayou charge?"

"We don't charge anything to Elders at

Dreamkeepers, but we don't publish books—certainly not *paper* books."

"Well, you WILL!"

AND SO, against all odds I might have given at the time, here is Edna's book *Voice of the Hawk Elder*—to my mind, an incandescent torch to light our way in these dark times.

Harvey Arden
September 2006

*What I see
I want you to see,
so that what you see
your children will be able to see,
and with Visionary eyes they will See.*

—Hawk Elder Edna Gordon

INTRODUCTION

We, the seeds of our ancestral traditions, have stood in the full circle of life to honor the Creator of all creations and a sacred bond with Mother Earth.

The Elders, messengers of Nature, have a responsibility to teach and to help prepare for Life's Earthwalk and the survival of the future generations.

A gathering can be any chosen path or spot where peace and contentment can be nourished, to become whole in body, mind, heart and spirit—and so to honor your mission in life.

Universal Awareness needs to be awakened to reinforce unity and equality to life in balance and harmony with all nations.

Y**ES, THIS IS MY VOICE**, and these are my words, my thoughts, my feelings, my opinions, my poems. My good friend Harvey has helped me sort and arrange'm, like he's done for lots of good people over the years, even back when he wrote for *National Geographic*. He fixes my spelling and he spruces up my grammar here and there, though I tell him, *not too much, Harvey*! I want folks to know who I am and how I really talk and what I'm really like. Don't make me sound like some saintly old lady come down from Heaven on a moonbeam spoutin' high-flown words.

 Me, I'm just me, Grandma Edna Gordon, Hawk Clan Elder of the Seneca Nation, Six Nations Iroquois Confederacy. I just turned 85, and I'm tryin' my darndest to be a good human being. Sometimes I succeed, but don't stay around me when I get mad! I turn into a raging hawk!

I **CONSIDER MYSELF** a native traditional Seneca Elder who stands within the circle of life, guided by the laws of the Creator and tied to the Earth like a child to the mother through the umbilical cord—never losing that connection.

 I'm honored Harvey's chosen me to work with. Or am I the one did the choosing? <smile> Harvey's a helper, and that's a holy thing to be. People'mselves aren't holy. But what they do can be holy. Living a holy life, that's what life's for. Helping others, fighting injustice, standing up for the People, saving our Mother the Earth—those are holy things to do.

 But always be sure to remember, it ain't *you*

yourself who's holy. People are just people. Harvey's no saint either! If God'd wanted folks to be holy, he'd have given'm wings and set'm up on a cloud somewhere playin' a big gold harp.

Sounds pretty boring to me. Me, I'd rather just be a human being. I'm thankful that's all I am or need to be.

Bein' human, that's a tough enough job for me.

USED TO BE I KEPT QUIET. I let my husband Hannibal do most of the talking. He was a spiritual leader of the Seneca Nation, though he wasn't a chief, just an ordinary man, a Wolf Clan Elder. When Hannibal talked, folks listened. He spoke from the heart and they listened from the heart. He changed their lives, like he changed mine. Hannibal made this world a better place, and that ain't easy to do.

Hannibal also wrote poems like me, and I include some of his poetry in these pages. To tell the truth, his thoughts and words are so mixed with mine I can hardly tell'm apart anymore. No matter. They're all one piece.

Now Hannibal's gone on ahead and left me here awhile to carry on alone—though my son Richard's always here for me, like his Dad was. So I've raised four kids, and helped with more'n a few grandkids as well. I love every one of'm for their own selves.

That's how we all need to be loved. That's how God, the Creator loves each of us. He created us and he loves us, each one of us for our own self.

SO WELCOME TO MY UMBRELLA TREE. Think of this whole book as an Umbrella Tree, just like the one in my backyard, a shelter and a refuge, a friendly place where you and I can sit and talk and get to know each other.

So go on, sit right there across the picnic table from me.

THERE'S more'n a little of me in each of these poems and in my spoken words that Harvey's set down along with the poetry. So when you're reading this book, you're reading me, too. We're in touch, we're in communion, you and me. That's a kind of holy thing, too. A miracle, really. That some black marks on paper stitch together you and me, your soul and mine. Yes, a true miracle—one of those countless true miracles we rarely even notice, rarely even acknowledge or appreciate.

THESE WORDS, these poems, these thoughts come to me like fallin' leaves driftin' into my lap. I study each leaf, each thought, then the autumn breeze carries'm away.

A few I write down, if I can remember'm. Others are gone forever. Once again, no matter. More'll be driftin' down into my lap any time now. There's always another breeze, and there's always another poem.

Here's a little leaf-poem that drifted into my lap one day not long ago when I was out walking in our meadow and a hawk flew out of the woods high over my head, making that high-pitched squealing sound they make.

It's a just a little poem, a very simple poem, but I like it. Some other leaf-poems follow.

SEEING WITH VISIONARY EYES

Take my hand, this weathered branch,
and walk with me along Life's Pathway
in this, my land, my sacred land.
I'll not lead….nor you.
Creator shows the Way.
Side-by-side we'll walk, just we two.
Yes, you and me. You'll see. You'll see.
With visionary eyes you'll see.
So don't be shy, dear friend.
Take my hand and let us make our visit.
Even now the spirits come, Creator-sent.
As we, too, are Creator-sent,
if we but knew.
Look there! A Hawk!
She flies before our eyes,
a red-tailed miracle.
She flies within us, too, you know.
Use your inner eyes
to see how she flies.

IT'S SAID that if you hear a hawk's cry and you remember to think of just what it was you were thinkin' right then, that there's a Sign in there for you. Hawk's cry is a Sign. Maybe an omen. Or an Instruction from the Great Spirit. That hawk's cryin' out to you to listen to your own self, to hear what you're your own Spirit is telling you!

WHEN YOU TAKE TIME to see a hawk, you're remembering Mother Earth, you're takin' time out for the Creator! If you travel in cars with Indian People, they're always seein' hawks and other birds up in the sky through the car windows. They call out, "Hawk! Hawk!"

They're connected.
And Creator hears them!

IF I HAD NEVER BEEN BORN

If I had never been born,
what would there be
instead of me?

A young girl? A yellow rose?
A hawk?

Oh, yes, a hawk!
A hawk there'd be
instead of me.

MOTHER EARTH'S ABUNDANT BLESSINGS

Mother Earth, with Spiritual values,
forever prods us to become aware
of a seed, blessed with life's miracle,
the rare beauty of a budding rose,
and bearing fruits along Nature's pathway.

She urges us to interpret the sound
of the wind, the ripples of the brook,
sweet harmony of a bird's song,
and faint rustling of falling leaves.

The Sun's living flames penetrate her soul.
The living waters quench her thirst.
The refreshing rains give nourishment.
The Four Winds vibrate with the Spirit of Life.

Mother Earth shares many great blessings,
Yet we the children of the Earth
take her precious gifts for granted.

PLACE OF FRIENDSHIP
(*Adeo' sha'*)

During our Earthwalk blessings shower us.
Miracles spring like flowers along our Path.

May our living light of love illuminate
our Brothers' and Sisters' beating hearts,
for Love Itself is the Path to Unity.

In the shelter of Creation,
within that Great Umbrella Tree of stars,
we realize—
we are loved by one another
and by Creator.
All is One.
All is Love.

SPELLBOUND

I am spellbound when my eyes
capture the height of a mountain.
I wonder, would my dreams reach so high?

If I could challenge the towering mountain
and look down into the valley below,
would I be satisfied with the green pastures?

When I follow a cool, winding brook,
I often ask, "Just where does it end?"
And I wonder, "How far in life could I go?"

I sit and listen to the lapping of the sea.
now peaceful, now angry,
like my heart within.

On the beach I find a shell and put it to my ear,
and within I hear roar of the whole ocean,
the roar of my own heart.

FACING THE WITHIN

You, who stand alone,
in thoughts of your own,
wish someone was there
to listen, or say words of prayer,
but, will someone listen,
when you refuse to listen Within?

You are a child at heart running
with the wind, inhaling a breath
of life within, and still, you are
running against the wind,
against the Within.

Once you face a raging wind
and truly listen Within,
the sun rises in your heart,
bringing a new Dawn of Peace
where your Destiny awaits.

MY ANCESTRAL PRIDE

I know who I was,
where I came from and why.
I clung stubbornly to my tribal land,
even though pierced
to the quick of my soul
by your lack of respect
for Creation.

I follow rivers, sun and wind.
I stand behind a huge rock, watching.
You're unaware I'm facing you,
high on a ledge, waiting
for your dubious plan for Mother Earth.
to unfold.

Will you dance as we danced
to renew the Earth?
Will you walk in balance and harmony
with Nature, as we walked, to thank her
for her precious gifts?

When I hear the echoes of an axe
and the crash of a fallen tree,
I curse your ways.
Though I be but a shadow,
I shall forever walk this land
where my ancestors before me
look up, weeping, from beneath the ground.

Will you remember them?
Will you remember me?

WINGS OF PRAYER

The Hawk and the
Wolf Spirit are united
as one in the Earthly
and Heavenly Garden
of the Creator.

One day, they will soar
together, protecting and guiding,
on wondrous Wings of Prayer.

WOLF SPIRIT OF WISDOM

We do not have a
mediator. Our conception
of the Great Spirit is to go
directly to the Creator in
spirit and truth, the same
spirit as the creatures, so
there may be a communion,
a sharing of feelings and
thoughts on your Earthwalk.

Walk, talk, and live
your dreams.
Don't be afraid
when old doors close
and new ones open.
Have faith
in the way things are.

HAWK TRAIL OF WISDOM

Yesterday
I was a raging Hawk,
swaying,
on life's pathway,
half-knowing,
night from day.
Yet thinking
I knew it all, dwelling,
on my own
beck and call.

Today,
I calmly face the Hawk
inside myself,
who flies
within my inner soul.
and leads me to
the heights of possibility

Tomorrow,
I pray, this Hawk
shall remain
steady,
as a gentle breeze,
peaceful,
as the waves
of the sea

Grateful, to walk
beside others
as one,
'neath the stars,
the moon
and the sun.

WORDS OF WISDOM
by Edwin Hannibal Gordon

It is not wise to smother the spiritual Light
that grows in the heart of a Brother.

Someone may really need the spark
that kindles the Heart of Another.

I SHALL REMAIN INDIAN
Written for (and with) Edwin Hannibal Gordon

In humble praise, O Great One,
I am thankful I was created an Indian.

I shall retain my dignity and identity.
I shall honor my ancestors
for they are responsible for my Earthwalk.

Therefore, in generations to come,
the ancients will be our foresight.

I shall stand proud
and remain myself,
an American Indian.

WOLFHAWK
Dedicated to Edwin Hannibal Gordon

We yearn to be One,
But we learn to be Two,
so we can be One again.

One Soul, One Heart,
Indivisible,
Me,
You
& Creator
—One Triple Unity!

O Loved One.
Even in Death,
No separation divides us.
Add, subtract, or multiply Our Souls,
we are eternally One!

Edwin Hannibal Gordon

"The more selfish you are the smaller your world becomes. You make yourself smaller by being selfish."

ACCEPT THE SHADOW-SIDE WITHIN

Deep in the well of the Soul
the shadow-side of yourself,
cries out for release.

Deep in the savage-side of the Soul,
your darkest Self sings your Death Chant.

Deep in the Soul's twilight,
where clouds are passing by,
and souls are marching on,
you pray, one day you, too, will belong.

Accept the shadow-side within;
Accept your whole Self.
Transform those inward demons
into the Warriors they are meant to be

For you are made of dark and light,
of sun and shadow, of good and, yes, of bad.
You need them all.
You are them all.

WE EACH CREATE, we each destroy, that's what that poem's all about. We're all part good, and we're all part bad, too. That's what bein' human's all about. The fight between the good and the bad inside of yourself is what we call Life.

In our Seneca tradition there's the Good Twin and the Bad Twin who helped create the world. And there's also a Good Twin and a Bad Twin inside each of us. We each got to come to terms with both of 'em, the good and the bad, to be whole human beings.

> *"The fight between the good
> and the bad inside of yourself
> is what we call Life."*

THERE'S THE DARK SIDE of yourself and there's the light side of yourself, the good side and the bad side, the kind side and the mean side. Ain't no way to get around it. We all got both. We got *all* those opposites inside us.

It's what we *do* with the good and the bad inside us that makes the difference between good people and bad, saints and sinners. It's each of our jobs as human beings to bring those two opposite sides together into One.

That doesn't mean goin' *with* the Bad Twin; it just means knowin' he's or she's there causin' trouble just when you least expect it. The Bad Twin keeps the Good Twin on his or her toes. You try to stay with the

Good Twin, but you always keep an eye on the Bad one too. You can be sure he or she's keepin' an eye on *you*, just waitin' for a chance to stir up trouble!!"

PEOPLE ASK ME, *"Do spirits and ghosts really exist? Is there a life beyond the grave?* Well, I tell them, when you yourself see and experience a Spirit, then you'll know.

I've had experiences like that. I'll tell you one.

Before my brother passed away, he was in a coma. We never thought he'd come out of it, but he woke up suddenly one day and blinked his eyes.

He said, "You know, *I was in another world!*"

Richard, my son, told him: "Yes, we know you was in another world."

He didn't say anymore. He had a smile on his lips, even though they were blue, and he leaned back and closed his eyes, and not long after that he passed to the other world. We call it the Skyworld.

So, you see, he was close to death, but his Spirit came here to be with us one last time.

AND THEN, after death, the Spirit comes, too. Like happened to me when I had Richard, right during his birth. I was really sick, deathly sick. The old folks said I was close to death, because I told'm I seen my Grandfather, who was long dead, standing there by the bed. I tried to go to him and take his hand. His lips were moving. He shook his head and waved his hands like this. He was tellin' me it wasn't time for me to go! And I tried to grab his hand because I felt so bad, so sick, *I wanted* to go! But he just faded away with a big silent "*NO!*" on his lips. And here I am more'n half a century later!

So that proved to me that there IS a SPIRIT, there IS something beyond there. That Skyworld's *real*!

A CHILD'S PRAYER

Nyah-weh[1],
for the feast we share.

Nyah-weh,
for blessings great or small.

Nyah-weh,
for the Great Spirit's tender care.

Nyah-weh,
for the love He gives us all.

1. *Nyah-weh* -thank you

CHILDHOOD'S THE BEST TIME. We grown-ups forget about miracles and wonders when we get older, but kids—Indian kids, white kids, black kids, every kind o' kids—live in the middle of a million miracles and wonders every day.

To kids the miracles and the wonders are natural as flowers growin' and birds flyin'. And they also see the flowers and the birds'mselves are miracles too! Everyday's a miracle and a wonder to kids. But we grown-ups, we teach'm to forget, teach'm not to see the miracles and wonders anymore. That's what kids get taught these days: *HOW TO FORGET!* Can you imagine that? Now what kind of so-called teachin' is that?

THESE DAYS, it seems, hardly anybody's teachin' the old ways, the real ways anymore. Today the Indian kids go to the government's schools and learn all American society's ways. They're taught White Man's language, and they're told their *own* language is no good anymore. They get punished if they even speak it at school. But your language isn't just a language, it's not just for talking to each other, it's YOUR WAY OF LIFE! Lots of Indian people grow up and don't even remember their own language anymore. They don't know how to speak to the Creator.

Now we've started some special Indian language schools so youngsters can learn their own language, even when it's not talked at home. There's an Indian language school like that for Seneca and other Haudenosaunee—that's Iroquois people—over in Steamburg, near here, and others up on Pine Ridge for

Lakota people—that's what you call Sioux—and lots of other places where Indians live.

The spirit of our People's *in* the language. It's our whole way of thinking about ourselves and about the world. The language you use is like the eyeglasses you see the whole Universe through. Put on someone else's glasses and you can't hardly see!

*"**We have to teach Creation itself to the children.**"*

MY MIS-MATCHED MOCCASINS

I look down at my moccasins.
What do I see?
They don't seem to match.
How can this be?

I have good woven moccasins,
but they don't seem to fit.
Why is one so far behind,
always out of step,
in the wrong direction?
One goes east, one goes west.
What must I do to get in step?

Let me run, let me escape,
Let me free my innerself.
I'll wear my moccasins with pride
and dance as One with the drumbeat!

Two mis-matched moccasins,
two mis-matched selfs.
And all become One in the Dance of Life!

IT'S A POPCORN-POTATOCHIP WORLD we're livin' in today. We got fast food for the stomach and fast food for the soul. Maybe don't nourish you, but it's quick and it's easy. Bet you never ate the REAL potato salad like we made in those days. Oh, my, it was the world's best meal all by itself! Nobody can seem to make that REAL potato salad today. Today kids think potatoes come instant or in chips in plastic bags or all greasy french fried like McDonald's or Burger King. They think corn comes popped with imitation butter on it, already salted! That's why I say it's become a *popcorn-potatochip world*.

It ain't real. It's all imitation.

I **THINK BACK** when I was a little kid livin' on a big farm—that was before we went to the orphanage. It was Depression times, and hard as it was and poor as we was, we had real treasures in those days. Natural treasures, not the bought'n kind. Our snacks didn't come in boxes or wrappers or silver foil—they were there for the taking!

I remember the little frozen apples we'd pick right out o' the snow in winter, and the dill pickles big as your whole forearm down in that old barrel in the root cellar out beside the house. Now *those* were treats. And they didn't rot your teeth like today's twinkies and goodbars and things. You didn't—you *couldn't*—buy'm in a cellophane wrapper down at the store, and, lemme tell you, gettin'm could be one real adventure!

THAT PICKLE BARREL now, that was a real challenge for little guys like us. My brother and me, we'd go down and sneak into the cellar. I remember that musty smell and the big barrel of pickles. We were so little we had to stand on a box or something just to see inside. And reachin' down up to our elbows into the briny pickle water to get one of those pickles, that could be downright dangerous! It's a wonder I never slipped and fell in there—or I'd be a pickle myself!

We'd hear my mother going around the house hollerin' for us and we could see her shadow but we wouldn't answer. Maybe we were little but we knew right and wrong, and we knew we weren't supposed to be down there. So we kept still and hid from her, sittin' there hidin' in the dark in that musty cellar and eatin' those giant pickles. Now that was fun!

AND, OH, those frozen little apples in winter! I remember one morning, me and my brother, we were real little, maybe four or five or so, and we went out huntin' those apples all by ourselves, the two of us. Those little shriveled apples, hidden there under the snow crust beneath the old apple trees, were worth way more to us than any old gold nuggets or Hope Diamonds, and when you found one and dug it out with your little fingers freezin' and your nails turnin' blue and, oh my! those were the best tastin' things in this whole World, better'n any ice cream or popsicle there ever was. Our tongues and our whole little mouths would go numb eatin'm.

O NE TIME, we were sittin' there in the snow eatin' those frozen apple miracles when all of sudden there was a beautiful white-tailed deer come out o' nowhere not ten feet away from us. Oh, she had a shiny black nose and big brown eyes so sad and human it was like she was about to say something to us. And in a way she did! She was lookin' at us eatin' our frozen apples there, and we were lookin' back amazed at her, and I don't know who was more fascinated, us or the deer!

The deer'd been eatin' the apples, too, but when we saw each other all of a sudden like that we all stopped chewin' and just stared. It's not like seein' a deer in a movie or a petting zoo or runnin' away from your car off a highway or strapped across some hunter's car-roof. This deer was *showin'* herself to us. That was the Great Spirit lookin' out at us from those big brown eyes. And that's true! And I knew she had exactly the same taste in her mouth as we did. The deer, us two kids, and the Creator all had that very same sweet cold wonderful frozen apple taste in our mouths! That's how Creator works! That was Nature, Mother Earth, teachin' us herself! We had front row seats on Creation itself! Now, you tell me about miracles!

T HEN WE'D RUN BACK to the house, and even when we were that little we'd help with whatever work was to be done. There was always big tasks for our little hands, like breakin' up bark for medicines, feedin' the chooks or the cows or the horses, or cuttin' beans. And yet there was a real *togetherness* when we did things like that, things that helped everybody, not just ourselves. It taught us *unity*! We were part o' somethin' much bigger than ourselves. We felt like we *belonged*!

And it taught us *un*selfishness. We learned the more unselfish we were, the better everything was. Yes, there was something more important than your selfish little self. There was the family, the community…and there was *everybody else*—the People!

WE LEARNED things only get worse for you when you're selfish. People're always forgettin' that. Bein' selfish hurts *everybody, EVEN YOU*!

The more selfish you are the smaller your world becomes. You make yourself smaller by being selfish.

NOWADAYS HUMAN BEINGS have lost touch with who we are, the children of this Mother Earth. We've lost touch with Creation itself. We see only our own little selfish tiny world. But we have to teach our children more than just about this little world of our own. We have to teach Creation itself to the children, show'm how they can find the whole of Creation in every leaf, in every flower, in every hawk that flies over their head with a Message from the Creator. We have to lead them into true wonder and true thankfulness for the Great Mystery of Creation, which we're each so lucky and privileged to be part of.

TAKE ADVANTAGE of this Life and this World you've been given. People grumble over the little things and forget all about Creation and the mysterious fact that *here we are right in the middle of it*! Now explain *THAT* to me! You can't! It's a Mystery, the greatest Mystery of all. The scientists, the astronomers, they'll never find it. Never ever! It'll always be a Mystery…because it's Creation itself! That's just the Way it is.

AND EVERYTHING about that Mystery is holy, sacred, wonderful, even if we don't notice it and grumble on about some little thing in our own selfish little life. It's only when you're selfish that Life seems little. If you're not selfish and you know how to share everything, you'll see how big Life can be. Life *IS* Creation. Life *IS* the World, the whole World, not just our little part of it.

WE DON'T ASK MUCH from the Creator, who already gives us so much more'n we could ever dream about prayin' for.

In our Way of Life, we give Thanks instead of always askin' for things. Some folks are always prayin' for this and prayin' for that. Ours is a 'Thank You' Way of Life. Maybe we ask for the safety and health of friends and loved ones, and for the blessing of living another day. But when that day comes, and we wake up into it, we give Thanks.

We give Thanks when the sun comes up in the morning. At night, we give Thanks for the night. Everything that was Created we give Thanks for.

To us, all of Life is a Thanksgiving!

I **BELIEVE** in another world, a better world. I believe in many worlds, as many worlds as there are places to put'm in all of Creator's Creation.

Creation's *much* **much** **MUCH** bigger than we think. It's so big the whole sky full of stars is just a tiny part of it. Creation's not just *out there*—it's here inside of ourselves, too. Each one of us *IS* a universe. Every molecule, every atom is a Universe, a World with still other Worlds inside o' that.

That's how Creation IS! It's so big in so many ways you and I can't even dream of it all.

BE A SHARER, be a giver, be a helper and the whole of Creation opens up around you and over you, like an Umbrella Tree. All of Creation is like an Umbrella Tree we live under—*really*, inside of, 'cause we ourselves our *part* of it!

That's the most wonderful thing of all, that we ourselves—even our selfish little selves—are *part* of that World, of that Creation, of that Umbrella Tree, of that Mystery!

Yep, that's the greatest thing of all, even if we go our whole lives and never even know it or realize that it's so. Whatever this great holy Mystery is, *we—each and every one of us*—are part if it! Be thankful for that. Stop askin' for little things. Just be grateful for that *Big Thing*. So send out a big thanks to Creation for makin' you part of Itself!

"We're all essential to Creation, each and every one of us."

LIFE IS A RIVER WE SWIM IN

Years it took me to return
to the riverbanks of O-he-yoh[2]
to recollect those childhood days of peaceful ways,
free as the birds and the wind.

Along the untrod bank
no campfire burned,
no ashes or debris
marred Creator's perfection.

This was Creation's very edge, and we were in it,
laughing and romping and splashing.

We whooped to hear our echo pierce the silence
of the Allegany rolling hills.

Our voices called back to ourselves,
speaking secret things
that only we could understand.

I'll tell you the secret of secrets.
Creator and Creation are One.

You don't need to think it;
just feel it in your Heart.

What the Heart knows,
the Mind will find reasons for.

2. *Upper Alleghany River, major tributary of the Ohio—or O-he-yo in the Seneca language.

THAT'S WHAT THE RIVER or the brook or the stream teaches us, if we just sit quiet on the bank and watch it flowin' by like Life itself. Life is a river. You got to learn to sit quiet on the banks of your own life as it flows on and on. You got to watch your life like it was a river, and see just how it's like that—flowing and meandering along, gettin' caught in a backwater or eddy, now you're in a rapids or even a whirlpool or—*oh, oh*!—there comes Niagara Falls, like we got just up north of here.

Life's like that, full of surprises and of all the unexpected obstacles it's gotta flow past or around or over. Life goes on like that, just like a river, and sooner or later we *ALL* go over the Falls! So don't tread water or thrash around like you're gonna drown, wavin' your arms so the lifeguard can see you.

There *ain't* no lifeguard!
So swim! Swim while you got a chance!

That's why I call that poem *Life Is A River We Swim In*.

WASTING TIME

You may call me a sinner
and curse these weary bones
as I sit and rock here,
'wasting time,'
just thinking,
just remembering,
just being.

Am I out of tune with life
to sit and sigh and dream a bit,
pondering years gone by?

I've often heard it said,
"Don't look back, live one day at a time."
But, oh, look back at times I must!
Have I left something undone?
a wound unhealed?
a hurt unsoothed?

Tears roll down my high-boned cheeks
from so much tragedy, so much pain
I've seen and felt and lived through.
But even as I weep
I smile an inward smile
for the blessings life also brings.

Good follows bad follows good.
That never changes.
That's Creator's Way.
Knowing that brings inner peace.

We don't leave the past behind;
we take it with us,
and it needs some tending, the past does.

Wasting time can sometimes—and I emphasize
sometimes—be the most important thing to do.

So sit and rock all you like when you're my age.
But don't forget to feed the dogs
and turn off the stove!

GIFTS WE SQUANDER

If the eyes were created to see,
Why are we blind to Creation's wonders?

If the ears were created to hear,
Why are we deaf to Nature's sounds
or to the voice of a brother in distress?

If the hands were created to be useful,
Why do we tolerate idleness?

If the feet were created to walk,
Why do we walk paths of pain and sorrow?

Creator's infinite gifts we squander,
and then ask for still more.

Don't be askin' so much of Creator.
Give thanks for all that's been given you.
Use what you got now instead of asking for more.

Give thanks for Creator's greatest gift to you
of all—the Gift of Life!

"If you don't know where you came from, how you gonna know where you're going?"

SIGNS OF LOVE

I often walk along a flowery path,
feeling the cool grass spring beneath my feet,
but when my sturdy moccasins falter
on the crooked pathways of Life,
I sense a watchful eye, somewhere above,
constantly warning me to follow the trail
marked with signs of Love.

When I'm faced with a troubled night,
I often become a fearful child.
I grope blindly for a guiding hand,
to lift me gently from my bended knee.
The precious Hand, not so very far away,
fills my soul with spirituality
and the power of Faith, to face another day.

If I am the target when poison words
pierce deep into the core of my inner self,
I keep smiling, remembering to place all
forgiveness within the church of my heart,
for in this sacred house of prayer
the door must forever be open,
so all the world can hear the
chant of Love within.
and know that Love is everywhere.

AN OLD WOMAN'S EARTHWALK

'Stay put, old woman!' they tell me.
'Get back in your rocker!"

But, old as I am,
Spirit calls me to an Earthwalk,
and an Earthwalk I take.

Autumn leaves pad my trail,
softening my footsteps,
easing the pain of old bones
whose spring, like mine, is gone.

To reach the hillside is a victory.
The hilltop would be a miracle.

The old man's not here to lean on anymore.
I lean hard on my weather-beaten cane.
When my bony knees feel too weak,
I just sit down.
Oh, I'm tired.
I hear myself wheezing.

Time was I would run these hills like a deer,
leaping and laughing and whooping.
Today I can only sit and try to smile.
And, yes, I do!
I smile at myself,
this old soul weather-beaten as my cane.

And I smile at memories
of Earthwalks past.
I stand among towering pines,
realizing how much I've shrunk!
Cheerful birds urge me on,
mocking me with their songs of youth.

Beside a brook I take off my moccasins,
and dip my bony old feet in the green ripples.
Oh, it's cold...and it tickles.
I hear myself laughing hilariously,
and the birds momentarily stop singing,
amazed at this silly old woman.

Somehow I reach the top,
breathless and wheezing,
but triumphant in my own little way.

Many seasons I've trudged this wise old hill,
always finding new discoveries,
new miracles.

I want to stomp and whoop
as I used to do on earlier Earthwalks
up this wise old hill.
But I'm much too tired.

I speak words of wondrous praise as,
face uplifted, arms held wide,
I pray to the listening sky.

Then down I must go,
before the night-owl hoots,

Down, down I pick my way.
'Don't fall, old fool!' I tell myself,
knowing the buzzards would pick my old bones
clean before anyone found me.

Then somehow I'm home again,
my body aching but my soul at peace.
I hang up my moccasins.
Now, they can say "Old woman, stay put!"

*"To free your innerself
is to be free
in mind and spirit.*

*May we follow only
the Way of the Great One,
no matter how difficult
the trail."*

AMERICAN SOCIETY'S tried to make it so we Original People hardly exist except as Tontos in the movies or as cigar store Indians. Well, me, I'm no cigar store Indian. I'm a **_HUMAN BEING_**. And I'm also an **_INDIAN_**, one of the Original People of this Earth. And I'm also a proud member of the Seneca Nation. We're just as much a Nation as your own United States, you know. We're *sovereign*, that's what it's called, just like every Nation. We got our own land and we got our own language and we got our own religion! How come we're not sittin' in the United Nations like you and all the other Nations? Where are the delegations from the Indigenous Peoples of the world? Don't we get even *one* seat?

WE INDIANS need to stop bad-mouthin' each other. Harvey here tells me first thing lots of Indians tell him, even when they hardly know him, is something trashy about some other Indian. We need to stop that! It's just dumb! That's just what the exploiters want—for us to be always fighting and squabbling with each other. And *hating* each other! Once we do that they can steal everything we got—and that's what they done and that's what they're still doin'!

So I tell people, Indian or otherwise, please find somethin' nice to say about some other Indian guy or gal or even a white guy or gal or whoever. Elsewise just bite your tongue, and don't say it *at all*. If you GOTTA say it, then be sure you say it right to the face o' the guy or gal you're sayin' it about! That's what a Warrior does!

Only wimpers go around badmouthin' someone who ain't there right then.

It's time we all did some *GOODMOUTHIN'* about each other!"

TO THE INDIAN YOUTH OF TOMORROW

I want you to see what I see,
so you will teach others
to see what you see.

Life, in all its forms,
is Creator's gift.
Take care of that gift,
for it's yours only a brief while,
then passes on
to future generations.

From a seed you were born,
and, if Creator wishes,
you'll grow strong and tall
into a Mighty Oak,
connecting Earth and Sky,
sheltering the People
beneath your spreading boughs.

Yes, a Mighty Oak you'll be
when you learn how truly to see
what a human being can be!

PEOPLE IN NEW YORK CITY turn on their air-conditioners and they got no idea how a whole world was destroyed so they can cool'mselves off. They don't know—or *care*—that many hundreds of our Seneca families were chased off their own ancient territory and made homeless by the so-called Kinzua Dam that makes their electricity.

To us it was a *'Death Dam.'* Death to a whole Way of Life.

My good Seneca friend Duce Bowen has gone around tellin' our Seneca young people what happened back there in the 60's and 70's when they started buildin' that dam. We need more teachers like Duce. Our kids need to learn what their own families went through back then—how their homes were bulldozed or left to drown, how their whole Way of Life was drowned.

Duce's writin' a whole book about it. He's a teacher, a real teacher of the real history of our People. He teaches the children and the People about where they came from.

If you don't know where you came from, how you gonna know where you're going?

I hope Duce's book wins one o' them Nobel Prizes. Then the World'll learn what happened on the Allegany Seneca territory. These days they call that kind of Injustice *"ethnic cleansing."* Imagine! They always got high-soundin' words for their crimes!

THESE government folks love puttin' dams on Indian land. And they love to cut their highways through Indian land. And to put their radioactive waste on Indian lands.

They're always glad to take another inch, another yard, another mile of what little's left to us of what Creator gave us.

But these little scraps of territory that they call 'reservations' is all we got! It's supposed to be *OURS*. All the treaties say you won't come and disturb'm, that they're ours as long as the sun shines and the rivers flow and the grass grows. That's what *your own government* wrote in your treaties—every one o' which you broke before the ink was dry!

Now with these dams you're takin' away the rivers themselves! And all the pollution'll blot out the sun completely one o' these days.

Yet you're always findin' some reason to come and take still more of our land away from us—*more* and *more* and *MORE!*

But your GREED's gonna kill the whole World!

Don't you care? Can't you SEE what you're doing?

A**ND THEN** they pour their poisons into our waters. Would you pour poison down your mother's throat? Well, that's what we're doin' with Mother Earth!

I don't understand how our so-called leaders just shrug their shoulders, and keeping makin' their big profits from their poisons.

They think Creation doesn't matter, Creator doesn't matter.

Well, they're wrong! Creation *DOES* matter!

Let'm make their money makin' the world clean again, not makin' it dirty!

SOMETIMES I wish someone'd *PULL THE PLUG* on that Kinzua dam! Oh, just imagine that, all that water goes floodin' downriver, leaving behind nothin' but mud and death and still more death. No, it can't be done, I know. You can't kill something and later make it live again. That old world's gone.

Or is it?

OH, MY HEART ACHES to tell you here, even as I'm writing these words, that DuWayne "Duce" Bowen, Seneca Elder, wonderful human being, my dear friend and fellow Warrior, has just passed this day on to that better world, the Skyworld, where the rivers still flow and the sun still shines and the grass still grows.

My tears dampen the page I'm writing on. What will happen to his book now? Just last week Duce sent me these words to include in this book. They're written for a future generation of our People...

A Reminder to Future Generations of My People
by DuWayne "Duce" Bowen

ON THE ALLEGANY INDIAN RESERVATION the Allegany Indian Reservation the U.S. government has posted a 'NO OCCUPANCY' sign on a third of the land—10,000 acres that have been unoccupied for a generation, since the land was flooded in 1972.

There's something our future generations should remember, and let this be a reminder from me...

Someday the dam at Kinzua will be no more!

Our Seneca fathers realized they couldn't stop the government from flooding our Allegany heartland. In their wisdom, they stipulated a proviso to which the U.S. government agreed. The Senecas kept the title to the land which the waters of Kinzua rest upon. We permitted a 'flowing easement' only.

Someday, when the waters of Kinzua are drained away, the land beneath remains Seneca Territory. It must be reclaimed by our People at that time.

Senecas...learn this and do not forget it!

It's possible that the government of the United States just might...just might...forget they had agreed back then to this fact.

It seems the government of the United States forgets easily.

Be sure to remind them, my future Brothers and Sisters, whose land this **is**—and whose land it shall remain **forever**!

THE BROTHERS walked slowly upon the abandoned road. They lived here at one time. They pointed to where the houses once stood. The schoolhouse stood over there. The graveyard was near there. Over there was the site of the old Presbyterian church. They looked down at Robinson Run as it ran its swift jagged course across the field, under the highway and into the river. They remembered the people, the homes, the times, and the mischief they once perpetrated there. They turned and walked away. They knew that the moon would rise tonight and shine on this land. They looked to the river and saw that it was still flowing. Overhead the sun shone brightly. All about them the grass was still growing.

This was just after the people were "removed" and before the floodgates closed to hold back the Allegheny River. The waters rose, drowning the old world beneath the Allegheny Reservoir. The government said the Seneca folks who were displaced would be "modernized." They said the new "lake" would make recreational "boomtowns" out of local towns like Kane, Bradford and Warren in Pennsylvania and Salamanca in New York.

But that "modernization" came with a tremendous price. The Old Ones, forced from their beloved homes and land, faded away rapidly. Sadly, they took with them their love, knowledge and strength.

Traditions, native knowledge, language and our Way of Life all died beneath the waters of Kinzua.

They moved displaced Seneca people into "new government Indian houses" that were so shoddily built they soon started falling apart. The prediction of "boomtowns" never materialized. Instead, local communities went into decline. Only sadness, tragedy and death were left for the Senecas who got chased out.

Every day orders are sent to Kinzua Dam to tell how much water to release that day so they can manufacture steel in Pittsburgh and have their airconditioners in New York City.

I wonder if those folks realize it's more than water that makes their steel and runs their airconditioners—it's Seneca blood.

~DuWayne "Duce" Bowen

A BROOMSTICK REVOLUTION

WE NEED CHANGES in this world, really big changes. I'm prayin' they'll be peaceable changes, not violent and bloody ones.

I'd like to see a peaceable revolution, a revolution of broomsticks instead of guns.

Call it a *Broomstick Revolution.*

That's right. The People pick up their broomsticks and march together and Sweep Injustice Out! Make a clean sweep, a big cleanin' like's never been seen before.

Broomsticks against Injustice. Now that'll be the day!

We'll take our broomsticks and we'll sweep Leonard Peltier right out o' prison, along with all the other innocents.

Yep—a *Broomstick Revolution!* That's what we need!

THERE'S AN INDIAN MAN I been writing to and he's been writing back to me. His name's Leonard Peltier, and he's for sure one of the finest human beings on this Mother Earth, even though he's sat in a prison cell for thirty years now. He was framed by the same people tryin' to frame *ALL* of us these days. Oil people. Energy people. Money people. Same kinda people who built that Kinzua Dam right here in the middle of our territory and drove us Seneca People off our ancient lands.

Same with Peltier's case. These energy folk wanted to steal the uranium on Indians' lands out west in South Dakota, just like they stole the gold and the coal and pretty much everything else. So they staged a shoot-out and then they framed Peltier to hide their own crimes. Same kind o' lies they're doin' all the time today with their wars and their so-called 'terrorists'. They called us Indians 'terrorists' too when we tried to defend our land.

Lies. Lies. **Lies!**

Fillin' their prisons with the innocent while the guilty run the country!

INJUSTICE is what these money people do best. Injustice is somethin' they've got lots of, and they sure given plenty of it to Leonard Peltier! Thirty years just for bein' innocent. Thirty years just for bein' Indian. And *still* they won't let him out.

These power people hate innocence. Maybe 'cause they sold theirs so long ago. And they hate Indians, too. That's 'cause we love our Mother the time

Earth and we don't want to see her raped!

So when I think of **In**justice I think of **Leonard Peltier**.

Maybe Jesus died for us all, like they say, I dunno. But I *do* know Leonard Peltier is sittin' in jail these thirty years for all of us Indian People, and *it's time we got him out*!

I **CRY** when I read Leonard's letters to me, knowing how many people beg him to write back and then get upset when he doesn't, and here he is sittin' in his cell writing to an old lady he don't even know!

He writes me: *"Dear Edna! Thank you very much for your good words about me in your New Year's message. Your words touched my heart and soul by this honoring....This year I am receiving a lot of good words from our Indian People, who say, 'Enough is enough! It's time for you to come home, Leonard! This is the year!' It makes me feel something is finally going to happen soon and I'll get out of this hell at last!"*

OH, I GOT TO CRY here all over again, 'cause he wrote this to me in 2003—already three more years've gone by. The only thing he got *out* of was Leavenworth. Now they sent him to Lewisburg prison in Pennsylvania, not so far from here, as it happens. Maybe I'll get to visit him there. I hope so.

Leonard's 62 years old now. He's been there in prison since he's 31. Imagine that! He's spent HALF his life in jail now for someone else's crime, somethin' he never did. And those FBIs and government people KNOW it, but they still keep him in there.

I say that's a terrible *terrible In*justice!

AS THESE WORDS are written, in July 2006, a terrible desecration is taking place at the holy mountain of so-called Bear Butte in the so-called Black Hills of so-called South Dakota. Our Lakota (Sioux) kindred out there are fighting to stop a big saloon and bikers' bar from being built right out in front of the Holy Mountain, where all the vision-questers and other folks will look down on it while they're praying.

This was where Crazy Horse prayed, and Sitting Bull, too, and a thousand generations of Indian people before them.

Harvey was just out there last month and saw it.

He writes: *"The saloon's frame is already up and building fast. It's the first thing people looking down from the mountain will see beyond a magnificent untouched prairie meadow—a sprawling, rowdy, ugly, neon-lit, noisy, beer-brawling, motorcycle-snorting desecration of a pristine wilderness.*

It truly sickens the heart."

WELL, I BELIEVE—I *hope*—Creator will strike that bikers' bar down with a vengeance. Indians and other folks are gathering there right now to protest and pray for intervention—if not by the Creator, then by the United States government! How can they let this abomination happen? Why don't all those bikers themselves stop swillin' beer for a while and join the People to stop this awful thing?

I JUST WROTE a poem I hope they can read to the protesters out there. Maybe this little prayer of a poem will catch their ear—or maybe even the ear of the Creator.

RESPECT TO AN ANCIENT MOUNTAIN

Sanctity of Bear Butte Mountain
was designed for Nature's perfection
by the hand of One Great Artist,
the Master Creator of All Creation.

The Spirit of the mountain,
a quiet place for meditation,
illumines the Spirit Within
to uphold our Sacred Tradition.

Mystic power of the Mountain
is there when all goes wrong,
and Someone Great stands by
to lend us strength.

You, brothers and Sisters -
you are today's Messengers.
We old ones pass that Message on to you.
Carry it well, like a flaming torch!

A Message to the Runners
World Peace and Prayer Day 2005
in the Black Hills, SD

I, Grandma Edna Gordon, Seneca Hawk Clan Elder,
of the Haudenoshaunee Iroquois Six Nations
Confederacy, personally commend and honour
each of you runners on your Spirit-run.

You have run for all of us.
You have run for each of us.
Your footsteps from the Four Directions
of Mother Earth
Are sacred and bless us all.

You bring the Four Directions here with you
to what Chief Arvol Looking Horse calls
"The Heart of Everything That Is" -
the sacred *Paha Sapa* or Black Hills.

Even as you runners have run the paths
of this Mother Earth for us,
so have you also run the great Sky Pathway
of the sun,
the wind, the rain, and the stars.
You have blessed us all
with your sacred footsteps.

Mitakuye Oyasin, as our Lakota relatives say,
We are all related. Yes, each and every one of us.

I **'VE BEEN HONORED** to have Lakota Chief Arvol Looking Horse, keeper of the Sacred White Buffalo Pipe, at my annual Hawk Elder Gathering here at Cattaraugus each fall. Arvol brings a special radiance to any occasion, and has opened sessions at the United Nations with moving ceremonial prayers, including sage, a Buffalo skull, and a lighted Pipe—or *Chanumpa*[3], as Arvol calls it (pardon my spelling), since he says it's too sacred to be called just a '*Pipe*.' The thousand-year-old Original Sacred White Buffalo Pipe he keeps hidden away in a safe place, but it was spiritually *still there* in Arvol's hand as he performed the UN ceremony with his personal *Chanumpa*. The UN personnel and every one else there was moved to the quick of their souls.

That Original *chanumpa*, we're told, is the source of power in all later chanumpas carried so proudly and reverently by many Indian Prayer-Warriors, or 'Pipe-Carriers,' to this day. Leonard Peltier carries one, and it's his proudest possession in that 5x9-foot concrete cell he's caged in—a 'house-guest in Hell' he's called himself.

That *chanumpa* keeps Leonard directly connected to Creator.

S**O, ANYWAY**, here I have this tall, regal, but modest and soft-spoken man—Chief Arvol Looking Horse himself—standin' in my little kitchen drinkin' that strong black coffee we drink and even laughin' at our bad jokes—that was one of the great honors of my life.

---

3. C'anupa (sacred pipe) is the spelling Chief Arvol uses in his book, *White Buffalo Teaching*s, though there are other spelling variations.

He spoke long and eloquent to our Gathering, encouraging us all to help him establish every June 21—the Summer Solstice—as an International Day of Peace and Prayer around the World.

And it's starting to happen in lots and lots of places in countries all around Mother Earth. Prayin' for Peace. All doin' it at once around the world. Creator'll be sure to hear.

Yep, Peace! That's the Holiest work of all in this World.

I **UNDERSTAND** Arvol is the 2006 recipient of the International Temple of Understanding Award, an honor previously given to the Dalai Lama and only a very few other world luminaries. I'm hoping he'll come up here for this year's Hawk Elder Gathering from New York City, where the award's given. We need his spiritual presence, and we've promised him all the hot black coffee and bad jokes he can take!

I'm also sending a special Prayer to the Creator here—a prayer I know Arvol joins us in. I'm prayin' just as hard as I know how that our Indian brother Leonard Peltier, now in Lewisburg Penitentiary just a few hours drive from here, will be mercifully released from his 30 years unlawful imprisonment and join us here along with Arvol.

Arvol and Leonard together! Right here at Cattaraugus! What a day that'll be!

That's gonna take a miracle, I know, but Prayer *CAN* work miracles, just like Arvol teaches in his book, *White Buffalo Teachings*!

77

And even if Leonard can't make it to our Hawk Elder Gathering this time, he's got a permanent invitation to be our guest next year or any year. And so does Arvol. Maybe even the Peacemaker Himself'll come to join us for such a sacred occasion. Leonard Peltier, Arvol Looking Horse, *and* the Peacemaker—all standin' here together in my little kitchen drinkin' that scaldin' black coffee and listenin' to our bad jokes!

Imagine! Keep prayin' for it. It *CAN* happen!

THE PEACEMAKER'S our People's Great Prophet and Lawgiver, just like Moses and Jesus in the Bible are to the Jews and Christians. He came to us a thousand-or-so years ago when we Haudenosaunee Peoples was all fightin' and killin' each other. The Peacemaker was born of a virgin mother, just like Jesus, over on the other side of Lake Ontario, not that far from here in what's now Canada, and He came across the lake in a miraculous white-granite Stone Canoe that He didn't have to paddle. It just took Him where he was supposed to go.

Travelin' in a canoe made out o' stone proved the Peacemaker was Creator's Prophet, sent into our world to make peace among the Five Nations—the Seneca, Mohawk, Onondaga, Oneida and Cayuga.

THE STONE CANOE took the Peacemaker up the rivers to each of the five original Haudenosaunee Peoples—first to the Mohawk, where he was joined in his sacred Peace-Work by Chief Ayawentha, or Hiawatha as some call him.

(Harvey tells me the poet Longfellow mistakenly set Hiawatha out West on the Mississippi in his famous poem *Hiawatha*; but he's really Haudenosaunee, and we still have a Mohawk Peace-chief who goes by that inherited name).

Together, the Peacemaker and Ayawentha traveled our rivers in their Stone Canoe, visiting each Nation and gettin'm to stop all that war and killin' and to join together in a Confederacy of Peace. They called it the Five Nations Confederacy—and for centuries they were the strongest Indian confederacy east o' the Mississippi, even long after the Europeans got here. They was also the most feared—and they established peace and order from up here in New York down to what's now Virginia and the Carolinas, and all the way westward across the land to the Mississippi River.

PEACEMAKER AND AYAWENTHA convinced the Five Nations to bury their hatchets of war under the Great Tree of Peace, and to come together in a Five Nations Confederacy. Much later, about the early 1700's, the Tuscarora People, from what's now North Carolina, got driven outta their land by the white folks, and they came up here—they already spoke a kind of our Iroquoian language—and joined our Confederacy to become the Sixth Nation. They're still not far from here.

Then, during your American Revolution, the Iroquois got tricked into fightin' on both sides, British and American, and lots escaped to Canada when the war was over. There's a big reserve called Six Nations up there in Ontario. Those are our People, too.

NOW I'M NO DARNFOOL. I have eyes. I see the world and all the Injustice that's going on in it right now. Injustice to Indian people. Injustice to indigenous Peoples. Injustice to the poor and the weak and the so-called 'developing' peoples all around this Mother Earth.

The *'Third World'—that's how they call it.*

But Mother Earth isn't the Third World. She's the FIRST world!

LOOK AT IRAQ. That's maybe the *BIGGEST INJUSTICE* they ever done since they tried to kill all us Indian people. But they *failed* when they tried to kill all us all, just like they'll *fail* in Iraq and anyplace else they invade with their bombs.

Creator's *against* us killin' each other. The killers'll *ALWAYS* be brought down! They may thump their chests now, but they're *comin' down* with a BIG BIG BUMP!

Remember Custer. He was a chest-thumper, too, but DOWN he came. Just like they all do. *Bump **BUMP BUMP! DOWN!***

You'll see. It'll happen.

Tell'm Hawk Elder, Grandma Edna Gordon told you so!

IT'S TIME we ended government Injustice in this land once and for all. We Indians knew it first, but this government has never stopped trampling other Peoples for it's own ends. The only ends a government should have is to help the People. Any ends beyond that should be declared illegal. Wars don't help the People. Wars kill the People—so how can they ***EVER*** be legal or so-called constitutional or ***right*** except in self-defense?

WE SAY we're fighting for Freedom, but Freedom for who? For you and me? Or for the Rich folks to be free to prey on the People? All these tax breaks the Rich, of all people, are getting these days. That's the People's money!

They think they can make money on the End o' the World!

But Creator's gonna step in, you'll see. He's gettin' mad! He's gonna stop the destruction of this World. But maybe we'll all die before He does it. That'll be our punishment, and it'll be well-deserved!

WHERE ARE all the people who'll stand up with me and say, "You STOP IT! No more Injustice!"

I'm sick in my heart at what we human beings have done - and keep doin' today - to Mother Earth and to each other and to the unborn generations still to come. It's all so unnecessary, and it's wrong, just plain *wrong* **wrong WRONG**!

Who's gonna stand up with me and SAY it to the government and to the whole World out there? You, Harvey? Or who??

Who's gonna stand up for the Creation?

SOMEBODY HAS TO STAND UP and fight and put this world in order. Just look at the turmoil going on in this world—all these earthquakes, the tsunamis, the hurricanes like Katrina, mudslides, glaciers melting, Global Warming, plus all the crazy people rattling their nuclear weapons. It's disaster on every side!

And there's all the sicknesses people are dying of these days—even people who led good lives. Diseases like cancer, diabetes, AIDS, and all that, and now they warn us Avian Flu is coming!

Creator's not causin' these things. Creator doesn't cause cancer. People cause cancer! Cancer hardly even existed before we poisoned the rivers and the air.

NOW WE SEE TREES DYIN' from the tops down, killed by our poisons. You know, that's part of the Iroquois Prophecies of a Changing Era—it's people who are causin' the End of their Own World. We have to stop that by stepping within the Circle Hoop of Life's existence, to acknowledge and to Honor the Greatest Eternal Cycle of All Life, Without Beginning, Without an End.

If we don't do this, who will? Isn't there anybody ready to stand up and fight to save the World, to save Mother Earth, to save Creator's Creation?

Maybe it'll be *you* who's reading these words! Yes, **YOU**!

That's why *each* of us, every one, is so important.

Because if just one of us stands up to fight all this evil, why—who knows? Maybe one more person'll stand up, then maybe another, then a few more, then lots of people start standin' up and after a while *everyone* stands up.

Then ALL HUMANITY stands up together! And we all cry out with one voice on June 21, Arvol's World Peace and Prayer Day—***"STOP THE INJUSTICE!"***

And it'll stop!

And it all started with one person! Look at Rosa Parks! It *can* be done! We *CAN* save the World. We, the children of Mother Earth, *WILL* unite as One!

WE CALL OUR INDIAN WAY the Good Way of Life. Livin' *with* Nature, not *against* Nature. Those money people like the Bad Way. All this bombin' and killin' in Iraq and other places—that's *the Bad Way of Death.*

We need to try Peace for a change.

Peace—that's the most powerful weapon of all.

What's the matter with Peace and Love and helpin' other human beings instead o' killin'm?

THE WHITE MAN, he invaded *our* country, too. He said he was a friend, but he stole our land. He said he came in Peace, and then he made War on us.

When *he* was hungry, we fed him and showed him how to find food. But when *we* were hungry, he let us starve. Killed as many of us as he could.

Now what kind of a Way is that?

YES, WE'RE ANGRY. But I say to our Indian People—let our anger be a healing anger, a peaceful anger, a loving anger. We need each other in this world. We even need our enemies. Enemies—or even just rivals—make you stronger and smarter and better Warriors.

The Creator sends each of us our enemies.

That's why Jesus said, 'Love your enemy'. Because your enemy makes you a stronger, better human being. Your enemies are Creator-sent, just like your friends.

We have best enemies just like we have best friends.

IT TAKES more courage to walk away from a fight than getting' into one. A Peace-Warrior needs the wisdom to stay out of a fight if it's possible. He or she needs to know how to fight in a peaceful way, a spiritual way, if we have to fight at all.

Peaceful Warriors—that's what we need!

SO WHAT CAN one person do in this violent world that's destroyin' itself before our eyes right now, this very day, this very hour?

You got to look for and find your own Inner Self. Yes, your Inner Self—it's right there inside o' you! It's *YOU* yourself! Nothin's more important than *livin'* from your Inner Self.

That's yours and yours alone. It's the deepest part o' your Soul, the part that connects up with Creation and doesn't get lost in the little things. I call it the Chapel of the Soul. It's the *Within of the Within*!

Let that be your refuge, your shelter, your own inner Umbrella Tree in these terrible times.

Stay connected to Creation! You yourself ARE that connection!

TO ALL READERS

Turmoils of Universal Law is a lack of communication. We are lost in the shuffle, away from the chosen path of birth for our mission of life.

We are a stranger of our inner-self. The wounds of the Earth and the wounds of the soul need to be healed.

We have torn the minerals from the soul of Mother-Earth and created a stagnant ripple of waters.

We are a part of each other and all our relations, the plants, animals, birds, fish and crawling creatures.

We need to face the problems and to exert our energy to learn, to grow and to direct our course to become our own Identity for the future generations to follow the Pathway of Peace.

OTHER WRITINGS OF EDNA GORDON

Out of the Ashes of the Past, The Wolf & the Hawk, Spirit of the Hawk, In Touch with All Creation, Survival of a Heritage, Chanting Song of the Hawk (Spirit of Life), Hawk Elder Speaks (Ancient Guideline for Wisdom), Long Struggle For Justice (Still Victimized), Crossroads of a Culture (Traditional Way of Life), Raging Hawk & Wisdom of the Wolf, Ancient Cultural Survival, Hawk Elder Speaks (On the Patterns of Life), Sacred Circle Fire of Peace (Dying Embers of the Past), Walking in Rhythm With Life, Inner Dimension of Peace (We Will Survive), Warning Song of the Hawk & Spirit of the Wolf, Tribute to a Rose (A Reflection of Life), Traditional Hoop of Love (Passion of the Soul), An Ode to Oheo (The Beautiful River), Gateway to the Soul (Traditional Earthwalk is to Unmask the Shadows of Your Inner Self), Soul Spirit of a Child, Soul Spirit of the Wolf (Nature's Law for Survival), Visions of the Hawk (Native Voice of an Earthwalk)

OTHER WRITINGS OF EDNA GORDON

Visions of the Hawk & Earth Wisdom (Reflecting Earth Law for Peace), To Walk With the Earth Is My Culture, Within the Garden Walls of Nature's Rustic Touch (a Poetic Adventure), Dawn of a New Day (A Cultural Revival to Walk with the Earth), Good Memories Live On Like Ripples of a Stream, Long Journey By Canoe & the Ever-Changing Era of peace, Hawk Trail of tears & Dust, Reflections of Piercing Arrows & Visions of Reality, Sacred Medicine Knowledge, Ancient reflections From the Windows of the Soul, 'Neath the Umbrella Tree (Fulfillment of Life), Seasonal Garden of the Soul (Poetic journey of Mind and Spirit), Seasonal Earthwalk (Life's Pathway), Soul Spirit of the Wind (Life's Pathway), Soul Spirit of the Living Waters (Life's Pathway), Wolf & Hawk Trail of Thoughts, Naturalistic Theme of Life & The Ever-changing Visions of Time, Traditional Earthwalk & My Roots of Wisdom, From a Seed to a Mighty Oak (A Reflection of Life)

Other books with Harvey Arden:

Author:
Wisdomkeepers: Meetings with Native American Spiritual Elders

Dreamkeepers: A Spirit-Journey into Aboriginal Australia

Travels in a Stone Canoe: The Return to the Wisdomkeepers

Have You Thought of Leonard Peltier Lately?

Editor:
Noble Red Man: Lakota Wisdomkeeper Mathew King

Prison Writings: My Life is My Sun Dance by Leonard Peltier

White Buffalo Teachings by Arvol Looking Horse

To order any of the previous books, please contact George Blitch: george@haveyouthought.com

or visit:

www.haveyouthought.com